Fox
Coloring Book

Get FREE printable coloring pages and discounted book prices sent straight to your e-mail inbox every week!

Sign up at:

www.adultcoloringworld.net

ISBN-13: 978-1530586219
ISBN-10: 1530586216

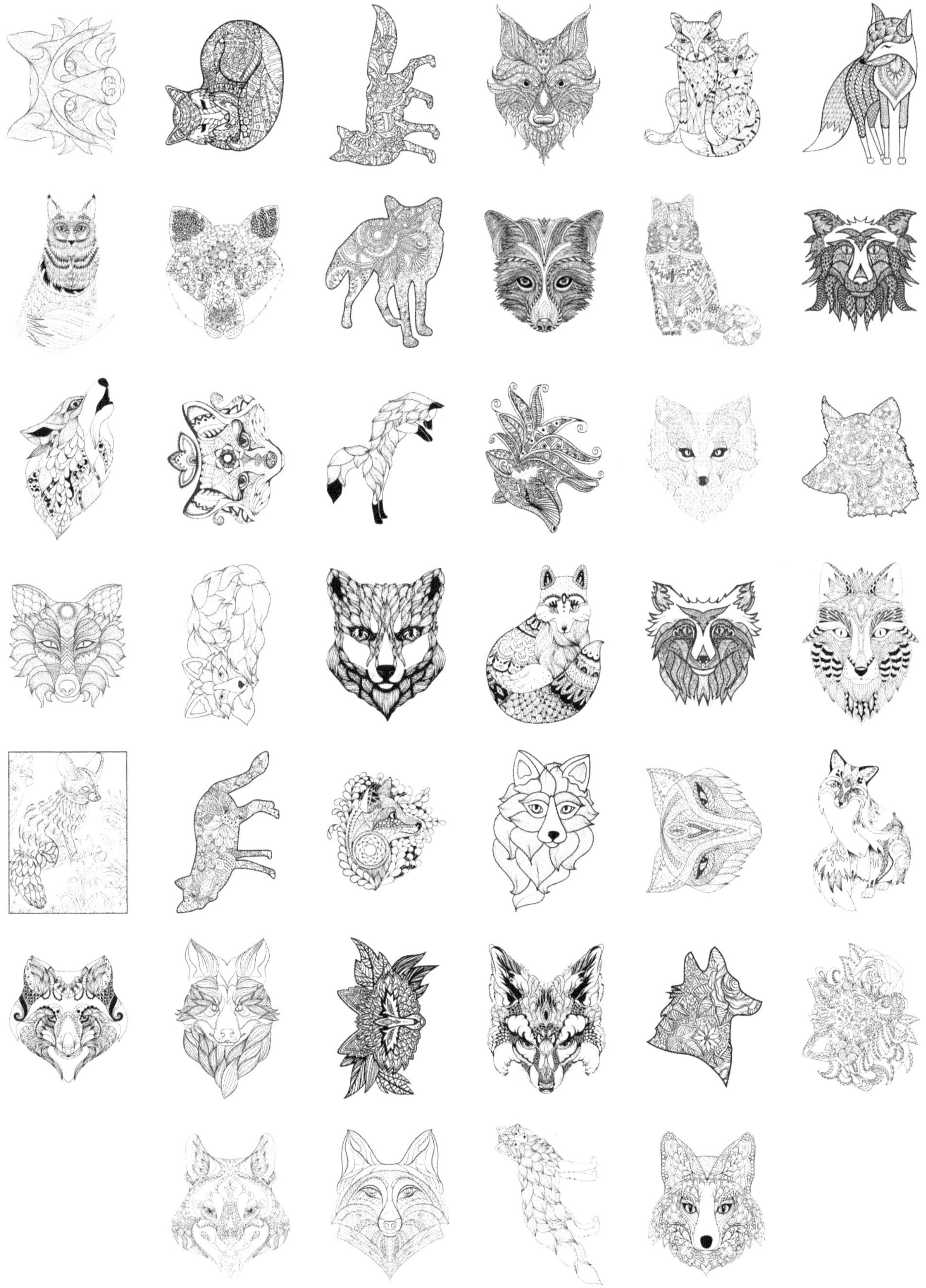

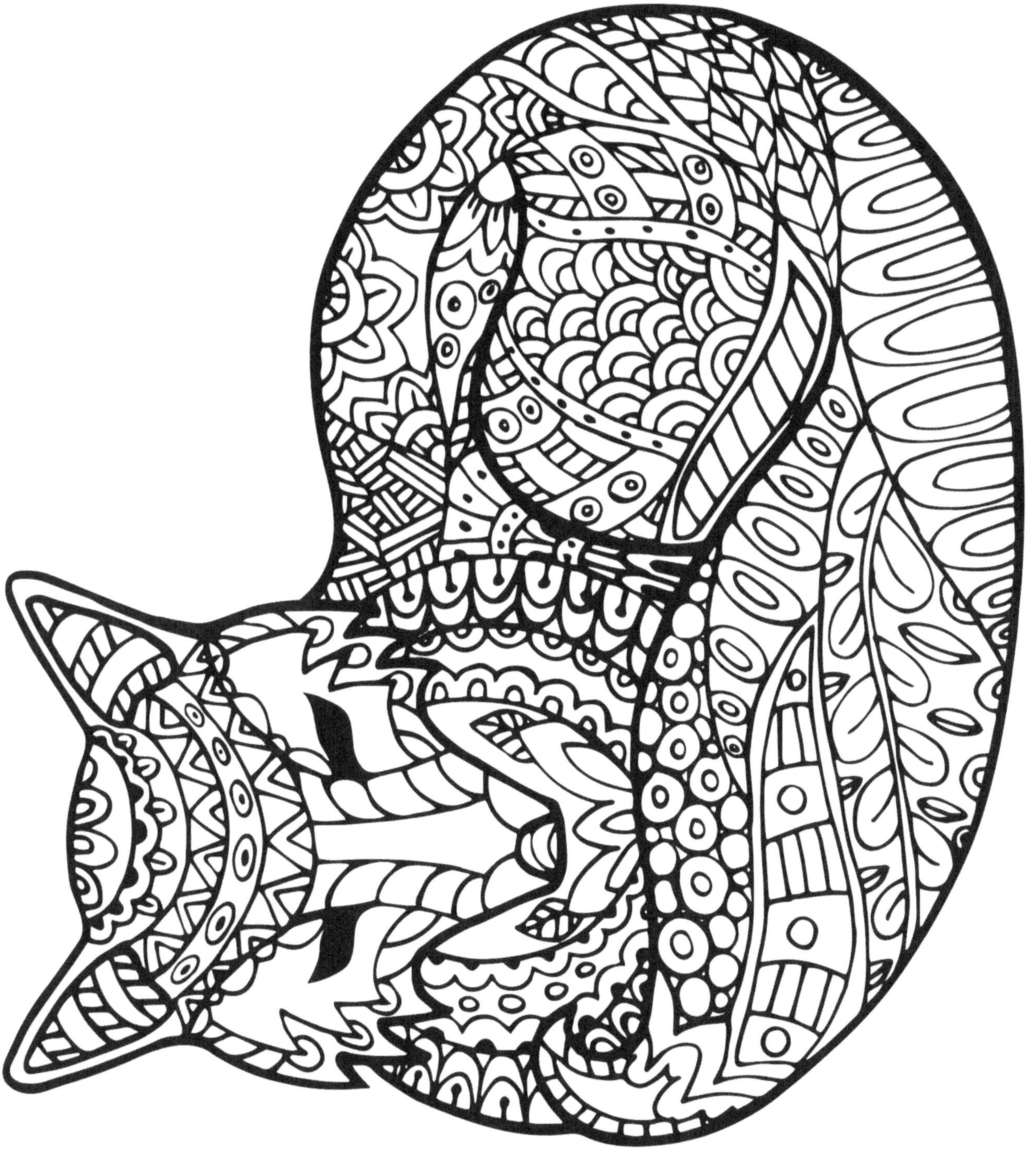

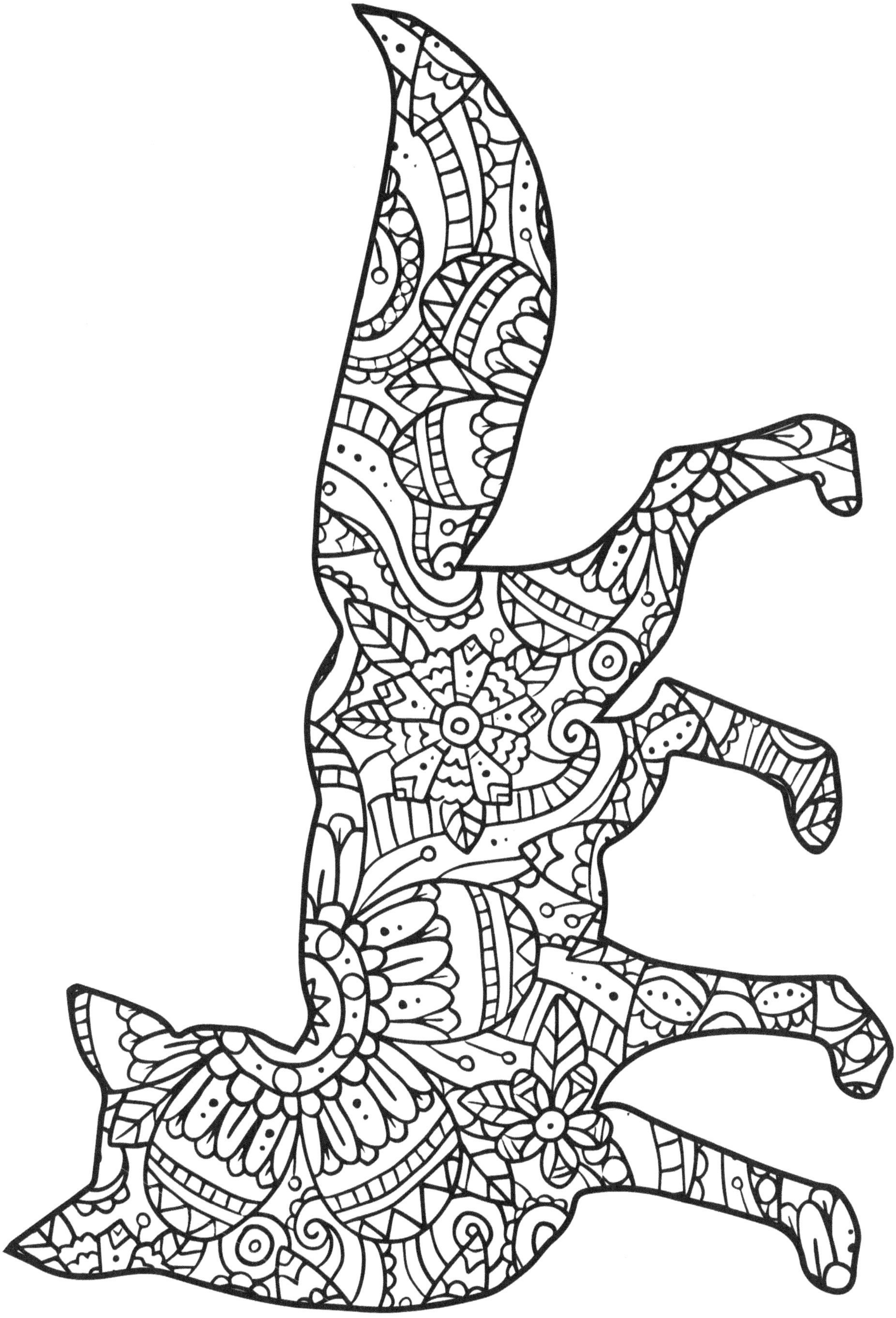

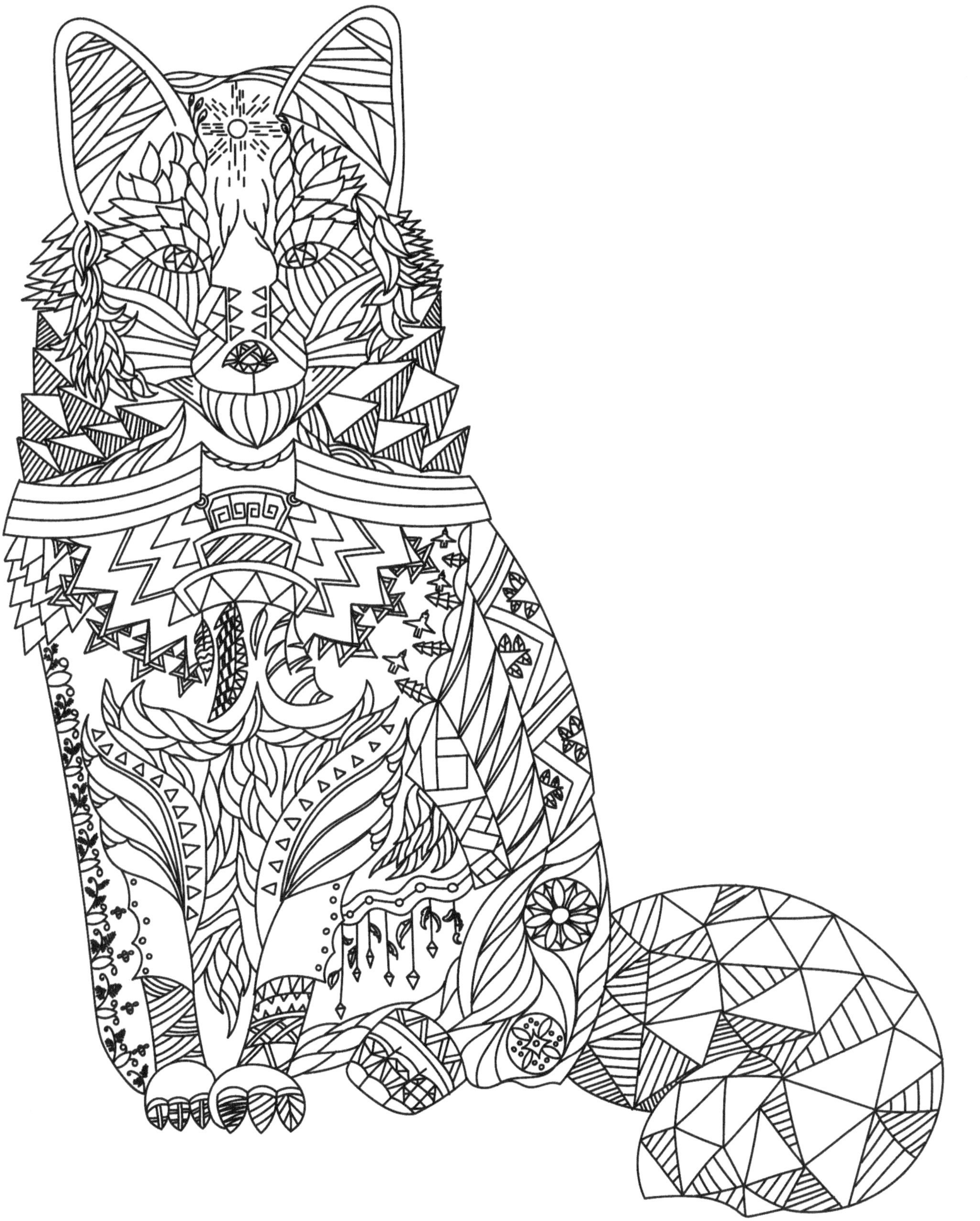

Color Test Page

Color Test Page

www.ingramcontent.com/pod-product-compliance
Lightning Source LLC
Chambersburg PA
CBHW081406280526
45788CB00009B/3008
* 9 7 8 1 5 3 0 5 8 6 2 1 9 *